Beginners Gui<

PAPER QUILTING

Comprehensive Step-By-Step Instructions To Mastering
The Art And Techniques Of Paper Quilting

Johnson Fisher
Copyright@2024

Table of Content

INTRODUCTION

Paper Quilting

Welcome to the enchanting realm of "Paper Quilting. In the pages that follow, we invite you to embark on a captivating journey where the age-old artistry of quilting intertwines with the imaginative world of paper crafting. Whether you are an avid quilter seeking a new medium for your creativity or a curious newcomer eager to explore the wonders of crafting, this book is your gateway to a universe of inspiring projects that seamlessly blend tradition with innovation.

As we delve into the intricate details of paper quilting, we'll unravel the secrets behind creating stunning pieces that capture the essence of quilted warmth using the versatile canvas of paper. From the basics of paper piecing to the more advanced realms of three-dimensional sculptures, our aim is to guide you through each step, fostering a sense of accomplishment with every completed project.

In these pages, you will discover not only the fundamental techniques of paper quilting but also a wealth of diverse projects designed to suit every taste and occasion. Whether you aspire to fashion intricate greeting cards, adorn your home with quilted decor, or engage in collaborative quilting endeavors, this book offers a treasure trove of possibilities.

So, with scissors in hand and creativity at the forefront, let's embark on this journey together. Happy quilting!

CHAPTER 1

Embarking on Your Paper Quilting Journey

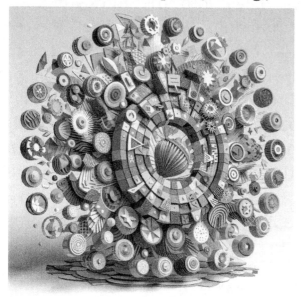

Welcome to the beginning of your adventure into the world of paper quilting! This chapter is all about preparing you for the creative exploration that lies ahead.

Introduction to Paper Quilting

Paper quilting is a creative craft that combines the principles of traditional quilting with the use of paper as the primary medium. In traditional quilting, fabric pieces are sewn together to create intricate designs and patterns. Paper quilting adapts these techniques to the unique characteristics of paper, offering a versatile and accessible way to explore quilt-like designs without the need for sewing or fabric.

In paper quilting, various types of paper, such as cardstock, scrapbooking paper, or specialty papers, are used to create layered and textured designs. Crafters often employ techniques like paper piecing, folding, cutting, and layering to assemble intricate patterns, reminiscent of traditional quilt blocks. The result is a visually striking piece of art that captures the warmth and charm associated with quilting.

This craft provides a creative outlet for those interested in exploring the world of quilting without the need for sewing skills or fabric materials. It allows for a wide range of artistic expression and experimentation with colors, textures, and patterns, making it an engaging and enjoyable craft for people of all skill levels.

Origins and Evolution of Paper Quilting

Paper quilting traces its origins to the time-honored tradition of quilting, a practice deeply rooted in various cultures around the world. Historically, quilting involved stitching together layers of fabric to create functional and often decorative textiles. The evolution of this craft has taken an intriguing turn with the introduction of paper as a primary medium.

Historical Roots:

The roots of quilting date back centuries, with evidence of quilted items found in ancient Egyptian tombs and medieval Europe. Early quilts served both practical and artistic purposes, showcasing intricate patterns and designs.

Influence of Traditional Quilting:

Paper quilting draws inspiration from the geometric precision and intricate patterns found in traditional quilting. It pays homage to the skillful craftsmanship of quilters throughout history, adapting their techniques to the unique qualities of paper.

Emergence of Paper as a Medium:

As paper gained popularity as a versatile artistic medium, crafters began exploring its potential in quilting. The lightweight nature of paper allows for intricate detailing and enables the creation of delicate designs that might be challenging with fabric alone.

Contemporary Fusion:

In recent decades, the fusion of traditional quilting principles with innovative paper crafting has given rise to a distinct form of artistic expression. Paper quilting offers artists and crafters a canvas to experiment with textures, colors, and three-dimensional effects, pushing the boundaries of conventional quilting.

Today, paper quilting stands as a testament to the adaptability and creative evolution of traditional crafts. This unique blend of history and innovation continues to inspire a new generation of artists, inviting them to explore the limitless possibilities that arise when quilting meets the delicate embrace of paper.

CHAPTER 2

Essential Tools and Materials

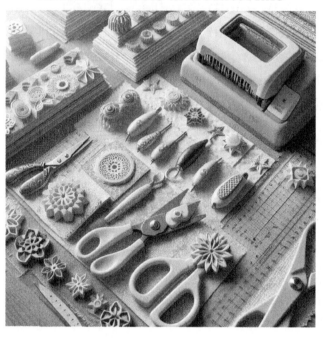

Embarking on your paper quilting journey requires a carefully curated set of tools and materials. Whether you're a seasoned crafter or a newcomer, having the right supplies ensures a smoother and more enjoyable creative process.

1. Quality Paper Selection: Invest in a variety of high-quality papers suited for your project needs. From textured

cardstock to patterned scrapbooking paper, having a diverse range allows for greater creative expression.

2. Precision Cutting Tools: Equip yourself with sharp scissors, rotary cutters, or precision knives. Precision is key in paper quilting, and these tools will help you achieve clean and accurate cuts.

3. Cutting Mat: Protect your work surface and extend the life of your cutting tools with a self-healing cutting mat. Its gridlines and measurements assist in achieving precise cuts and measurements.

4. Rulers and Templates: A variety of rulers and templates, including square, rectangular, and specialty shapes, will aid in creating consistent and intricate patterns. They are indispensable for achieving symmetry and precision.

5. Adhesives: Choose archival-quality glues or double-sided tape suitable for paper crafting. Ensuring your adhesives are acid-free will help preserve your creations over time.

6. Bone Folder: A bone folder is a handy tool for scoring and folding paper with precision. It helps create crisp, clean lines, particularly crucial in paper piecing.

7. Tweezers: Fine-tip tweezers assist in handling small and delicate paper pieces. They provide control and accuracy, especially when working on intricate designs.

8. Embellishments and Markers: Explore a collection of embellishments such as stickers, markers, or ink pads to add personal touches and details to your paper quilting projects.

9. Storage Solutions: Organize your tools with storage containers or a crafting caddy. Staying organized will enhance your workflow and prevent frustration during your creative process.

As you gather these essential tools and materials, you're laying the foundation for a seamless and enjoyable paper quilting experience. Each item is important and plays a crucial role in bringing your creative vision to life. Happy crafting!

Choosing the Perfect Paper

Selecting the right paper is a crucial step in ensuring the success of your paper quilting projects. The texture, weight, and pattern of the paper will significantly influence the final outcome.

1. Consider Paper Weight: Choose paper with an appropriate weight for your project. Heavier cardstock provides stability for intricate designs, while lighter paper may be suitable for more delicate and airy creations.

2. Texture Matters: Explore papers with different textures to add depth and visual interest to your quilting. Smooth surfaces offer a clean and polished look, while textured papers can evoke a tactile and dimensional feel.

3. Patterned or Solid Colors: Decide whether you want to work with patterned paper, solid colors, or a combination of both. Patterned paper can introduce a

dynamic element to your quilting, while solid colors offer a more traditional and cohesive look.

4. Consider the Theme: Align your paper choices with the theme or inspiration behind your project. Whether it's a seasonal design, a specific color palette, or a particular motif, let the theme guide your paper selection.

5. Acid-Free for Longevity: Opt for acid-free paper to ensure the longevity of your creations. Acid-free paper prevents yellowing and deterioration over time, preserving the quality of your paper quilts.

6. Experiment with Specialty Papers: Explore specialty papers like vellum, metallic, or handmade paper to add variety and uniqueness to your projects. These papers can introduce interesting textures and visual effects.

7. Coordinating Colors: If your project involves multiple pieces, ensure that the colors of your chosen papers coordinate harmoniously. A well-thought-out color

scheme enhances the overall aesthetic of your paper quilting.

8. Test Before Committing: Before diving into a larger project, conduct small tests with your chosen papers. This allows you to see how they interact, ensuring that your final creation aligns with your vision.

By considering these factors, you'll be equipped to make thoughtful and creative choices when it comes to selecting the perfect paper for your quilting endeavors. Enjoy the process of exploring different textures and colors, and let your chosen papers bring your vision to life. Happy quilting!

Setting Up Your Creative Space

Setting up your workspace for paper quilting is a crucial step to ensure an organized, efficient, and enjoyable crafting experience. Here's a guide to help you create a workspace tailored to your paper quilting needs:

1. Choose a Well-lit Area: Select a workspace with good natural or artificial

lighting. Proper lighting is essential for accurate cutting, precise folding, and overall visual clarity.

2. Invest in a Sturdy Table: Use a sturdy and spacious table as your crafting surface. Ensure it provides enough room for your paper, tools, and projects without feeling cramped.

3. Protect the Surface: Place a self-healing cutting mat on your worktable. This not only protects the table surface but also extends the lifespan of your cutting tools by providing a smooth and resilient cutting area.

4. Organize Tools: Arrange your essential tools within easy reach. Keep scissors, cutting tools, rulers, and other frequently used items nearby to streamline your workflow.

5. Storage Solutions: Invest in storage containers or organizers to keep your workspace clutter-free. Caddies, drawers, or bins can help categorize and store various papers, tools, and embellishments.

6. Dedicated Spaces for Different Tasks: Designate specific areas for different tasks. For instance, create a cutting station with your cutting mat and tools, a folding area, and an assembly zone where you'll put together your paper quilt pieces.

7. Comfortable Seating: Choose a comfortable chair that supports good posture. Since paper quilting can involve intricate work, having a comfortable seating arrangement is essential for extended crafting sessions.

8. Inspiring Decor: Personalize your workspace with inspiring decorations, such as artwork, color schemes, or motivational quotes. A visually appealing and inspiring environment can enhance your creativity.

9. Adequate Ventilation: If you're using adhesives or other crafting materials with strong odors, ensure proper ventilation in your workspace. An open window or a small fan can help keep the air fresh.

10. Keep Safety in Mind: Ensure that your workspace is safe. Store cutting tools

securely, keep cords organized, and be mindful of fire hazards if you're using heat tools.

11. Multifunctional Workstation: Consider a multifunctional workstation if you have limited space. Foldable tables or crafting desks with built-in storage can help maximize your available area.

Remember that your workspace is a reflection of your creativity, so tailor it to suit your preferences and needs. By setting up an organized and comfortable space, you'll create an environment that enhances your paper quilting experience and encourages a flow of creative ideas.

CHAPTER 3

Mastering Fundamental Techniques

Now that you have your tools and the perfect paper, let's delve into the fundamental techniques that form the backbone of paper quilting. These techniques lay the groundwork for creating intricate and visually stunning quilted designs.

1. Paper Piecing Basics: Choose a simple paper piecing pattern for beginners.

Print or trace the pattern onto the backside of your chosen paper.

Cut out the paper pieces, leaving a small margin around the edges.

Begin with the central piece and layer subsequent pieces, adhering them precisely using glue or double-sided tape.

Press down gently to secure the pieces together, forming a cohesive design.

2. Folding Techniques: Select a square or rectangular piece of paper for folding practice.

Experiment with basic folds like mountain folds, valley folds, and accordion folds.

Combine different folds to create more intricate patterns and textures.

Practice precision in your folds to achieve clean and well-defined lines.

3. Precision Cutting: Choose a sharp pair of scissors, a rotary cutter, or a precision knife.

Align your paper on the cutting mat and use rulers or templates for straight cuts.

Practice cutting curves and intricate shapes, maintaining accuracy.

Experiment with different cutting tools to find the one that suits your preferences.

4. Assembling Paper Pieces: Lay out your cut paper pieces in the desired pattern on your workspace.

Follow the order of assembly based on your chosen design.

Apply glue or double-sided tape to the edges or back of each piece.

Carefully align and adhere the pieces together, ensuring precision in placement.

5. Creating Intricate Patterns: Start with a simple pattern and gradually progress to more complex designs.

Break down intricate patterns into smaller, manageable sections.

Work on one section at a time, ensuring each part is accurately assembled.

Combine different shapes and patterns to create your unique designs.

6. Scoring and Folding Lines: Use a bone folder or scoring tool to mark folding lines on your paper.

Place the ruler or template along the desired fold line to guide your scoring tool.

Apply gentle pressure and run the scoring tool along the line to create a visible indentation.

Fold along the scored lines, using the bone folder for crisp and clean folds.

7. Balancing Colors and Textures: Experiment with different paper types, colors, and textures.

Create a color palette that complements your overall design.

Balance vibrant and subdued colors to achieve a harmonious composition.

Consider the visual weight of each element to create a balanced and visually appealing quilt.

8. Experimentation and Iteration: Try various combinations of techniques to discover your preferred style.

Allow yourself to make mistakes and learn from each iteration.

Don't be afraid to experiment with unconventional materials or methods.

By systematically practicing these steps, you'll develop proficiency in each basic paper quilting technique. Over time, these skills will contribute to the creation of intricate and visually captivating paper quilt designs.

Advanced Techniques

1. Layering and Collage: Select multiple papers with varying textures and colors.

Cut out shapes or patterns from different papers.

Layer the cut pieces, experimenting with various combinations.

Use adhesive foam dots or other dimensional adhesives to create a 3D effect.

2. Intricate Folding Patterns: Choose a larger piece of paper for more complex folding.

Explore advanced folding patterns like tessellations or origami-inspired folds.

Utilize scoring tools to create precise folding lines.

Experiment with symmetry and asymmetry in your folding designs.

3. Quilled Paper Elements: Cut thin strips of paper in various colors.

Roll the strips tightly to create quilled shapes.

Experiment with different quilling techniques, such as tight coils, loose coils, and scrolls.

Adhere the quilled shapes onto your paper quilt for added texture.

4. Incorporating Fabric Elements: Integrate fabric pieces into your paper quilt design.

Use fabric as a background or for specific elements within the paper quilt.

Secure fabric pieces with fabric glue or double-sided tape.

Experiment with the juxtaposition of paper and fabric textures.

5. Transparency Effects: Choose translucent or vellum paper for added transparency.

Overlay transparent elements onto your paper quilt design.

Experiment with layering transparent papers to create subtle depth.

Pay attention to how light interacts with the transparency for unique effects.

6. Embossing and Debossing: Select sturdy paper for embossing or debossing.

Use embossing folders or embossing pens to create raised textures.

Experiment with heat embossing for added dimension.

Incorporate debossing techniques by pressing the paper into textured surfaces.

7. Paper Marbling: Explore the art of paper marbling using water or shaving cream.

Drop ink or paint onto the surface and create unique patterns.

Press your paper onto the marbled surface to transfer the design.

Allow the marbled paper to dry before incorporating it into your quilt.

8. Interactive Elements: Integrate interactive components, such as movable parts or hidden pockets.

Create flaps, folds, or rotating mechanisms within your paper quilt.

Ensure that the interactive elements are securely attached for durability.

As you delve into these advanced techniques, approach each step with patience and creativity. Experiment with different combinations and modifications to make these techniques uniquely yours.

CHAPTER 4

Troubleshooting and Tips

Troubleshooting is an integral part of any crafting process, including paper quilting. Here's a guide to help you troubleshoot common issues that may arise during your paper quilting projects:

Inaccurate Cuts

Issue: Cuts are uneven or not as precise as desired.

Troubleshooting: Ensure your cutting tools are sharp.

Use a self-healing cutting mat to provide a smooth cutting surface.

Double-check your measurements before cutting.

Consider using rulers or templates to guide your cuts.

Paper Warping

Issue: Paper becomes warped or curled.

Troubleshooting: Avoid excessive use of wet adhesives that can cause paper to warp.

Use lightweight papers for intricate folding to minimize warping.

Allow glued layers to dry under a weight to prevent warping.

Adhesive Mishaps

Issue: Glue shows through or doesn't adhere properly.

Troubleshooting: Use minimal amounts of glue or opt for clear, archival-quality glues.

Ensure your paper is dry and clean before applying adhesive.

Experiment with double-sided tape for cleaner results.

Folding Difficulties

Issue: Difficulty achieving crisp and clean folds.

Troubleshooting: Use a bone folder or scoring tool for precise folding lines.

Score your paper lightly before folding.

Practice on scrap paper to refine your folding technique.

Pattern Alignment Issues

Issue: Difficulty aligning paper pieces in intricate patterns.

Troubleshooting: Use templates or rulers to maintain pattern alignment.

Cut pieces slightly larger than needed to allow for adjustments.

Double-check the placement before securing pieces with adhesive.

Color Bleeding

Issue: Colors bleed or transfer unexpectedly.

Troubleshooting: Choose papers with minimal ink saturation.

Test papers for colorfastness before using.

Avoid excessive use of wet adhesives on papers that bleed easily.

Overly Complex Designs

Issue: Feeling overwhelmed with the complexity of the design.

Troubleshooting: Start with simpler projects and gradually progress to complex designs.

Break down intricate patterns into smaller, manageable sections.

Take breaks to avoid fatigue and maintain focus.

Difficulty with Interactive Elements

Issue: Interactive components not functioning as intended.

Troubleshooting: Ensure moving parts are securely attached.

Test interactive elements during the assembly process.

Consider simplifying or reinforcing complex interactive features.

Storage and Organization

Issue: Difficulty keeping materials organized.

Troubleshooting: Invest in storage containers, caddies, or organizers.

Label storage solutions to easily locate materials.

Establish a habit of cleaning up and organizing after each crafting session.

Creative Block:

Issue: Feeling stuck or uninspired.

Troubleshooting: Take a break and step away from your project for a while.

Explore new techniques or styles to reignite creativity.

Seek inspiration from other artists, online communities, or nature.

Remember, troubleshooting is a natural part of the crafting process. Embrace challenges as opportunities to learn and improve your skills. Each issue you encounter and resolve contributes to your growth as a paper quilter.

General Tips

1. Start with Simple Projects: If you're new to paper quilting, begin with straightforward projects to build your skills and confidence before tackling more complex designs.

2. Invest in Quality Tools: Use high-quality cutting tools, adhesives, and paper to achieve cleaner and more professional results.

3. Practice Precision: Pay attention to precision in cutting, folding, and assembling. Small details make a significant difference in the final outcome.

4. Organize Your Workspace: Make sure you keep your workspace tidy and organized. A well tidied environment enhances creativity and focus.

5. Experiment with Papers: Explore a variety of papers, including different textures, weights, and patterns. It adds depth and also interest to your designs.

6. Learn from Others: Join online communities, attend workshops, or follow tutorials to learn from experienced paper quilters and gather new ideas.

7. Embrace Mistakes: View mistakes as learning opportunities. Don't be afraid to try new things, and don't get discouraged if a project doesn't go as planned.

8. Test Before Committing: Before using a new paper or technique in your main project, conduct small tests to see how it behaves and ensure compatibility.

9. Explore Mixed Media: Incorporate other artistic elements like watercolor, ink, or colored pencils to enhance your paper quilting designs.

10. Balance Color and Texture: Pay attention to the balance of colors and textures in your designs. You can experiment with different combinations to create appealing compositions.

11. Customize Patterns: Modify existing patterns or create your own to add a personal touch to your paper quilting projects.

12. Take Breaks: Avoid burnout by taking breaks during extended crafting sessions. This will help you to maintain focus and prevents you from getting fatigued.

13. Protect Your Tools: Keep your cutting tools sharp and well-maintained to ensure clean and precise cuts.

14. Share Your Work: Share your creations with friends, family, or online communities. Constructive feedback can provide valuable insights and encouragement.

15. Stay Inspired: Find inspiration in various sources, including nature, art, and everyday life. Inspiration can strike at unexpected moments.

16. Document Your Progress: Keep a crafting journal or take photos of your projects at different stages. This allows you to track your progress and reflect on your creative journey.

17. Enjoy the Process: Embrace the creative process and enjoy the act of crafting. The joy of creating is as important as the finished product.

Paper quilting is a versatile and evolving craft, so feel free to adapt these tips to suit your personal style and preferences.

CHAPTER 5

PROJECTS

Quilted Greeting Card

Materials:

- Blank card or cardstock folded in half

- Colored or patterned paper (scraps work well)

- Glue or double-sided tape

- Scissors

- Ruler (optional)

Steps:

1. Prepare Your Card: Start with a blank card or fold a piece of cardstock in half to create your card. Ensure that the card is well-creased for a clean fold.

2. Cut Paper Squares: From your colored or patterned paper, cut small squares. These can be uniform in size or vary for a more eclectic look. Aim for around 1 inch (2.5 cm) squares for a standard-sized card.

3. Arrange Your Design: Before gluing anything down, play around with the arrangement of your paper squares on the card. Experiment with different patterns, colors, and orientations until you find a design you like.

4. Glue the Squares: Once you've settled on a design, start gluing the squares onto the card. You can use a small dot of glue on the back of each square or apply double-sided tape.

5. Create a Quilt Pattern: Aim to create a quilt-like pattern by arranging the squares in rows or a patchwork style. You can

alternate colors, create diagonal patterns, or experiment with a random arrangement.

6. Consider a Border: If you like, create a border around the edge of the card using a contrasting color or pattern. Cut strips of paper and adhere them around the perimeter of the card for a finished look.

7. Trim Excess Paper: If any paper squares extend beyond the edges of the card, use scissors to trim them for a neat and polished finish.

8. Optional: Add Embellishments: Enhance your card by adding additional embellishments such as stickers, small paper shapes, or even a stamped greeting.

9. Personalize the Inside: Don't forget to personalize the inside of the card with your own message or a thoughtful greeting.

10. Let it Dry: Allow your card to dry completely before handling or delivering it. This ensures that the paper squares are securely adhered.

Feel free to experiment with different color schemes, patterns, and arrangements to make each quilted greeting card uniquely yours.

Paper Quilt Bookmark

Materials:

- Patterned scrapbooking paper

- Cardstock or heavier paper

- Glue or double-sided tape

- Scissors

- Ruler

Steps:

1. Select Materials: Choose a variety of patterned scrapbooking papers and a sturdy cardstock or heavier paper for the base of the bookmark.

2. Measure and Cut the Base: Decide on the size of your bookmark. A standard size is around 2 inches by 6 inches (5 cm by 15 cm). Cut the cardstock or heavier paper to your desired dimensions.

3. Cut Strips from Patterned Paper: Cut thin strips (about 0.5 inches or 1.5 cm wide) from your patterned scrapbooking paper. These will be the "patches" for your quilted design.

4. Arrange Strips on Base: Start arranging the strips on the base, experimenting with different patterns and colors. You can create a traditional quilt pattern or go for a more random arrangement.

5. Glue or Tape Strips in Place: Once you're satisfied with the arrangement, use glue or double-sided tape to secure the strips onto

the base. Ensure that each strip is adhered well to prevent peeling.

6. Trim Excess Strips: If any strips extend beyond the edges of the base, use scissors to trim them, creating a neat and tidy finish.

7. Add Embellishments (Optional): Enhance your bookmark by adding extra elements like small paper shapes, stickers, or even a ribbon at the top for a decorative touch.

8. Create a Border (Optional): If you like, create a border around the edges of the bookmark using a contrasting color or pattern. Cut strips of paper and adhere them around the perimeter.

9. Personalize the Bookmark: Consider adding a personal touch by incorporating a stamped message, a quote, or the recipient's name onto the bookmark.

10. Allow it to Dry: Let your paper quilt bookmark dry completely before handling or using it. This ensures that the strips are securely attached.

11. Laminate (Optional): For added durability, you can laminate the bookmark. This protects it from wear and tear and makes it more resilient.

Feel free to experiment with different patterns, shapes, and color combinations to create unique paper quilt bookmarks.

Mini Paper Quilt Wall Art

Materials:

- Canvas or sturdy paper

- Assorted colored paper or scrapbooking paper

- Glue or double-sided tape

- Scissors

- Ruler

Steps:

1. Prepare Your Canvas: Start with a canvas or sturdy paper. Choose a size that suits your space and preferences. Ensure the canvas is clean and ready for your design.

2. Cut Colored Paper Squares: Cut small squares from your colored or scrapbooking paper. Aim for squares around 1 inch (2.5 cm) in size. You can choose a color scheme or go for a more eclectic mix.

3. Arrange Your Design: Before adhering anything, play around with the arrangement of your colored paper squares on the canvas. Experiment with different patterns, shapes, or even try creating an abstract design.

4. Glue the Squares: Once you're satisfied with the arrangement, start gluing the colored paper squares onto the canvas. Use a small amount of glue on the back of each square or opt for double-sided tape for a cleaner finish.

5. Create a Quilt-Like Pattern: Aim to create a quilt-like pattern by arranging the squares in rows or a patchwork style. You can experiment with alternating colors, creating diagonal patterns, or even making concentric shapes.

6. Consider a Border: If you like, create a border around the edge of the canvas using a contrasting color or pattern. Cut strips of paper and adhere them around the perimeter for a finished look.

7. Trim Excess Paper: If any paper squares extend beyond the edges of the canvas, use scissors to trim them for a neat and polished finish.

8. Optional: Add Texture or Layers: Experiment with adding texture or layers to your mini paper quilt. Consider incorporating elements like fabric, ribbon, or other textured materials for added interest.

9. Personalize the Artwork: Add a personal touch by incorporating a stamped message,

a quote, or even your signature onto the canvas.

10. Allow it to Dry: Let your mini paper quilt wall art dry completely before handling or hanging it. This ensures that the colored paper squares are securely adhered.

11. Frame (Optional): If desired, frame your mini paper quilt wall art for a polished and finished presentation.

12. Hang and Enjoy: Your mini paper quilt wall art is now ready to be hung and admired. Find the perfect spot to display your handmade creation and enjoy the vibrant and textured design.

Feel free to experiment with different color schemes, patterns, and arrangements to make each mini paper quilt wall art uniquely yours.

Quilted Coasters

Materials:

- Cardstock or heavy paper

- Mod Podge or clear sealant

- Foam brush

- Colored or patterned paper

- Scissors

- Ruler

Steps:

1. Prepare Your Base: Cut squares from cardstock or heavy paper to serve as the base for your coasters. A standard coaster size is around 4 inches by 4 inches (10 cm

by 10 cm), but you can adjust based on your preference.

2. Cut Colored Paper Squares: Cut smaller squares from colored or patterned paper. Aim for squares around 1 inch (2.5 cm) in size. Choose a color scheme that complements your decor.

3. Arrange Your Design: Before adhering anything, experiment with the arrangement of your colored paper squares on the coaster base. Create patterns or go for a random and eclectic look.

4. Apply Mod Podge or Sealant: Using a foam brush, apply a thin layer of Mod Podge or clear sealant to the coaster base. This will act as both adhesive and sealant for the colored paper squares.

5. Adhere Colored Paper Squares: Press the colored paper squares onto the coated coaster base in your chosen arrangement. Ensure that each square is securely adhered.

6. Seal the Top Layer: Once the colored paper squares are in place, apply another

thin layer of Mod Podge or sealant over the entire surface of the coaster. This will seal the top layer and provide a protective finish.

7. Trim Excess Paper: If any paper squares extend beyond the edges of the coaster, use scissors to trim them for a neat and polished finish.

8. Optional: Add Embellishments: Enhance your coaster by adding extra elements like stickers, small paper shapes, or even a layer of glitter for a decorative touch.

9. Allow it to Dry: Let your quilted coasters dry completely before handling or using them. This ensures that the colored paper squares are securely attached and the sealant is fully dried.

10. Set of Coasters: Repeat the process to create a set of matching coasters. Experiment with different color schemes or patterns for a diverse set.

11. Protect Surfaces: Use your quilted coasters to protect surfaces from hot or cold beverages. They add a touch of handmade charm to your living space.

Feel free to experiment with different colored papers, patterns, and arrangements to create coasters that match your personal style and decor.

Simple Paper Quilt Journal Cover

Materials:

- Plain journal or notebook

- Assorted colored paper or scrapbooking paper

- Glue or double-sided tape

- Scissors

- Ruler

Steps:

1. Select Materials: Choose a plain journal or notebook as your base. Consider the size and style that you prefer.

2. Measure the Cover: Use a ruler to measure the dimensions of the journal cover. This ensures that your paper quilt design will fit perfectly.

3. Cut Colored Paper Squares: Cut small squares from colored or scrapbooking paper. Aim for squares around 1 inch (2.5 cm) in size. Choose a variety of colors or stick to a specific color scheme.

4. Arrange Your Design: Before adhering anything, experiment with the arrangement of your colored paper squares on the journal cover. Consider creating patterns, gradients, or a random arrangement.

5. Apply Glue or Tape: Once you've settled on a design, apply glue or double-sided tape to the back of each colored paper square.

6. Adhere Colored Paper Squares: Press the colored paper squares onto the journal cover in your chosen arrangement. Ensure that each square is securely adhered.

7. Create a Quilt-Like Pattern: Aim to create a quilt-like pattern by arranging the squares in rows or a patchwork style. You can experiment with alternating colors, creating diagonal patterns, or even making concentric shapes.

8. Optional: Add Borders or Frames: Consider adding borders or frames around the edges of the journal cover. Cut strips of paper in a contrasting color and adhere them to create a finished look.

9. Trim Excess Paper: If any paper squares or borders extend beyond the edges of the journal cover, use scissors to trim them for a neat finish.

10. Personalize the Cover: Add a personal touch by incorporating a stamped message, your name, or any other embellishments that resonate with you.

11. Allow it to Dry: Let your simple paper quilt journal cover dry completely before handling or using the journal. This ensures that the colored paper squares are securely attached.

Feel free to experiment with different color schemes, patterns, and arrangements to create a journal cover that reflects your personal style and creativity.

Advanced Projects

Quilled Paper Artwork

Materials:

- Colored paper strips in various widths and colors

- Quilling tool

- Canvas or heavy paper

- Adhesive (glue or quilling glue)

- Precision scissors

- Clear sealant (optional)

Steps:

1. Gather Your Materials: Collect a variety of colored paper strips. Experiment with different widths and shades to add depth and dimension to your quilled artwork.

2. Prepare the Canvas: Choose a canvas or heavy paper as the base for your artwork. Ensure it's clean and ready for your quilled design.

3. Experiment with Quilling Patterns: Use your quilling tool to experiment with various quilling patterns such as tight coils, loose coils, scrolls, and marquise shapes. Create a few sample shapes to understand how they will work together.

4. Plan Your Design: Sketch or plan your design on the canvas. Consider the

placement of different quilled elements and how they will come together to form the final artwork.

5. Quill Your Elements: Start quilling your chosen shapes according to your design. Keep your coils tight and secure by applying a small amount of adhesive at the end of each strip. Experiment with shaping the coils to add dimension.

6. Assemble the Design: Begin attaching the quilled elements to the canvas, following your planned design. Use adhesive to secure each quilled piece in place. Allow the design to evolve organically as you work.

7. Layering and Dimension: Experiment with layering quilled elements to create depth. Consider overlapping coils, arranging shapes in clusters, or creating a central focal point for added dimension.

8. Refine and Adjust: Fine-tune your design as needed. Trim any excess paper strips or adjust the placement of quilled elements to achieve the desired composition.

9. Seal the Artwork (Optional): If you want to protect your quilled artwork and give it a polished finish, consider applying a clear sealant. This will also enhance the colors and provide durability.

10. Frame Your Quilled Masterpiece: Once your quilled artwork is complete and dry, consider framing it to showcase your intricate and detailed paper quilling.

11. Experiment with Color Variations: Try creating different versions of your quilled design by using different color schemes. Play with complementary colors, monochromatic tones, or even gradient effects.

12. Share and Display: Display your quilled paper artwork proudly in your home or share it with others. Consider gifting your creation to someone special or participating in art exhibitions to showcase your quilling skills.

Creating quilled paper artwork is a meticulous and rewarding process that allows for endless creativity. Experiment with shapes, patterns, and color combinations to make each piece uniquely yours. Enjoy the artistry of paper quilling!

Mixed Media Collage

Materials:

- Various papers (textured, patterned, vellum, etc.)

- Fabric scraps

- Acrylic paints

- Gel medium

- Canvas or mixed media paper

- Brushes

- Palette knife

- Found objects (optional)

- Stamps and ink pads (optional)

Steps:

1. Prepare Your Canvas or Paper: Choose a canvas or mixed media paper as your base. Consider the size and orientation that suits your vision.

2. Gather a Variety of Materials: Collect an assortment of papers, including textured, patterned, and vellum papers. Also, gather fabric scraps, acrylic paints, and any other materials you'd like to incorporate.

3. Create Background Texture: Apply a thin layer of gel medium to the canvas using a palette knife. While the medium is still wet, press various textured papers onto the surface to create an interesting background. Allow it to dry.

4. Incorporate Fabric Elements: Cut or tear fabric scraps into interesting shapes. Apply more gel medium to the canvas and adhere the fabric elements, layering them for added texture.

5. Integrate Acrylic Paints: Use acrylic paints to add color to your collage. Experiment with blending, layering, and creating interesting color combinations. Give it time and allow the paint to dry between layers.

6. Add Dimension with Stamps (Optional): If desired, use stamps and ink pads to add patterns or textures to your collage. This can enhance the visual interest of the piece.

7. Layer Found Objects (Optional): Incorporate found objects, such as small trinkets or interesting items, into your collage. Adhere them with gel medium for a three-dimensional effect.

8. Experiment with Composition: Play with the arrangement of elements on your canvas. Consider balance, contrast, and focal points as you build the composition.

9. Create Depth with Layering: Use gel medium to layer papers and fabric elements, creating depth within your collage. Overlapping elements can add visual interest and complexity.

10. Fine-Tune and Adjust: Step back and assess your collage. Make any necessary adjustments, add or remove elements, and ensure that the composition aligns with your artistic vision.

11. Seal the Collage: Once you are satisfied with the composition, seal your mixed media collage with a clear sealant to protect the layers and enhance the vibrancy of the colors.

12. Frame or Display: Decide whether you want to frame your mixed media collage or display it unframed. Select a framing option that complements the style and size of your artwork.

Feel free to experiment and let your creativity guide you in creating a one-of-a-kind piece of art!

Paper Marquetry Art

Materials:

- Colored and patterned paper
- Craft knife or precision cutter
- Wood panel or thick paper
- Adhesive (glue or mod podge)
- Pencil
- Ruler
- Clear sealant (optional)

Steps:

1. Select Your Materials: Choose a variety of colored and patterned papers for your

marquetry design. You should consider color palettes that align with your style.

2. Prepare the Base: Decide on the size of your artwork and prepare a wood panel or thick paper as the base. Ensure it's clean and smooth.

3. Design Your Marquetry Pattern: Sketch your marquetry pattern on the wood panel or paper using a pencil. Consider intricate geometric shapes, floral patterns, or any design that inspires you.

4. Cut Paper Strips: Using a craft knife or precision cutter, cut paper strips in various colors and patterns. The width of the strips will depend on your design, so experiment with different sizes.

5. Create Marquetry Elements: Cut the paper strips into smaller pieces to form the individual elements of your marquetry design. Aim for precision in cutting to achieve clean and accurate shapes.

6. Arrange the Elements: Begin arranging the cut paper elements on the wood panel according to your design. Play with the

placement of colors and patterns to create a visually appealing composition.

7. Glue the Elements: Apply adhesive (glue or mod podge) to the back of each paper element and carefully adhere it to the wood panel. Ensure each piece is securely attached.

8. Layering and Detailing: Experiment with layering the paper elements to add depth to your marquetry design. Consider creating intricate details and patterns by overlapping and interlocking the pieces.

9. Fine-Tune Your Design: Step back and assess your marquetry artwork. Make any adjustments or fine-tune the arrangement to achieve a balanced and harmonious composition.

10. Seal the Artwork (Optional): If you want to protect your paper marquetry art and enhance its longevity, consider applying a clear sealant. This will also add a subtle sheen to the finished piece.

11. Let it Dry: Allow your paper marquetry artwork to dry completely before handling

or framing. This ensures that the paper elements are securely adhered to the base.

12. Frame or Display: Decide whether you want to frame your paper marquetry art or display it unframed. Choose a framing option that complements the style and size of your artwork.

13. Share Your Art: Share your paper marquetry art with others. Consider exhibiting it in art shows, sharing it on social media, or gifting it to someone special.

Paper marquetry art offers a unique and intricate way to create beautiful designs with the versatility of colored and patterned paper.

Interactive Paper Sculpture

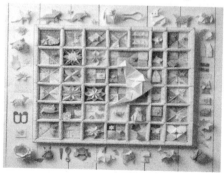

Materials:

- Cardstock or heavy paper
- Scoring tool
- Craft knife or precision cutter
- Brads or small fasteners
- Decorative paper or embellishments
- Glue or double-sided tape
- Ruler

Steps:

1. Select Your Materials: Choose sturdy cardstock or heavy paper for the base of your interactive paper sculpture. Gather decorative paper or embellishments for added details.

2. Create the Base Structure: Cut the cardstock or heavy paper into the desired shape for your sculpture. This could be a simple geometric shape or a more intricate design. Consider the theme or concept you want to convey.

3. Score and Fold: Use a scoring tool to create fold lines on the cardstock. These will be the hinges for your interactive elements. Score along the lines where you want the paper to bend easily.

4. Cut Out Interactive Elements: Using a craft knife or precision cutter, carefully cut out interactive elements from the scored areas. This could include rotating parts, pop-ups, or movable components. Ensure that the elements are connected to the base.

5. Decorate and Enhance: Decorate each interactive element with decorative paper or embellishments. Add colors, patterns, and details to make the sculpture visually appealing.

6. Attach Brads or Fasteners: Insert brads or small fasteners through the scored and cut areas to allow movement of the interactive elements. Make sure they are secured tightly to allow smooth motion.

7. Ensure Smooth Movement: Test the movement of each interactive element.

Ensure that they rotate, pop up, or move smoothly without any restrictions.

8. Add Additional Details: Enhance your interactive paper sculpture by adding additional details such as small paper shapes, textures, or even tiny decorations that complement the overall theme.

9. Secure Loose Ends: Use glue or double-sided tape to secure any loose ends or excess paper that may interfere with the movement of the interactive elements.

10. Fine-Tune and Adjust: Step back and assess your interactive paper sculpture. Make any necessary adjustments, refine the details, and ensure that the overall design is cohesive.

11. Personalize Your Sculpture: Add a personal touch by incorporating a message, a story, or thematic elements that convey meaning. Consider the narrative aspect of your interactive sculpture.

12. Display or Share: Decide whether you want to display your interactive paper sculpture as a standalone piece or

incorporate it into a larger art project. Share it with others to showcase your creativity and craftsmanship.

13. Document the Mechanism: If you've created a complex interactive mechanism, consider documenting the process or mechanism for others to understand how your sculpture works.

Creating an interactive paper sculpture allows you to explore movement and engagement in your artistic expression.

Layered Papercut Shadow Box

Materials:

- Colored paper or cardstock in various shades

- Craft knife or precision cutter

- Shadow box frame

- Adhesive (glue or double-sided tape)

- Foam adhesive dots or squares

- Pencil

- Ruler

- Cutting mat

Steps:

1. Select Your Materials: Choose a shadow box frame that suits your preferred size and style. Gather colored paper or cardstock in various shades for the layers of your paper cut design.

2. Prepare the Design: Plan your paper cut design by sketching it on a piece of paper. Consider creating multiple layers with intricate details to add depth to your shadow box.

3. Cut Out the Base Layer: Use a craft knife or precision cutter to cut out the base layer of your design from a single sheet of

colored paper. This layer will be the background of your shadow box.

4. Create Additional Layers: Trace the base layer onto different colored paper and cut out additional layers. Each layer should have distinct elements that contribute to the overall design. Experiment with varying shapes and sizes.

5. Add Details to Each Layer: Enhance each layer by adding intricate details through papercutting. This could include patterns, motifs, or even tiny scenes. Take your time to achieve precision in your cuts.

6. Layer the Cut Elements: Use adhesive (glue or double-sided tape) to layer the cut elements on top of each other. You can now arrange them strategically to create depth and dimension. Consider using foam adhesive dots or squares to elevate certain elements for a 3D effect.

7. Assemble the Shadow Box: Open the shadow box frame and place the layered papercut design inside. Ensure that the

layers are properly aligned and secured within the frame.

8. Secure Layers in Place: Apply a small amount of adhesive to the back of each layer before securing it in place. This ensures that the layers remain fixed within the shadow box.

9. Fine-Tune the Arrangement: Step back and assess the arrangement of layers. Make any adjustments to achieve a balanced and visually pleasing composition.

10. Optional: Frame the Exterior: If desired, add an additional layer to the exterior of the shadow box frame by cutting and adhering colored paper or decorative elements.

11. Personalize and Detail: Add any additional personalized touches or details to the papercut layers. This could include tiny figures, words, or symbols that hold significance.

12. Seal and Protect (Optional): If you want to protect your layered papercut design from dust and damage, consider

spraying a clear sealant over the entire piece. This also adds a subtle sheen to the paper.

13. Display Your Artwork: Place your layered papercut shadow box in a prominent location where it can be admired. Consider incorporating it into your home decor or gifting it to someone special.

Creating a layered papercut shadow box allows you to play with dimension and intricacy, resulting in a visually captivating piece of art.

CONCLUSION

The journey into the world of paper quilting projects has been an exploration of creativity, craftsmanship, and artistic expression. From the humble origins of paper quilting to mastering advanced techniques, this book has aimed to inspire and guide you through a variety of projects that showcase the beauty and versatility of paper as an artistic medium.

Through this book, you've discovered the joy of transforming ordinary paper into extraordinary works of creativity. Whether you're a seasoned paper quilter or a novice exploring this craft for the first time, the projects within these pages are meant to inspire, challenge, and ignite your passion for paper quilting.

As you continue your artistic journey, remember that each piece you create is a reflection of your unique perspective and creativity. Cherish the process, embrace experimentation, and most importantly, let your imagination guide you. The world of paper quilting is vast and ever-evolving, offering endless possibilities for self-expression and artistic growth.

May your future projects be filled with inspiration, innovation, and the joy that comes from turning simple sheets of paper into intricate works of art. Happy quilting!

Printed in Great Britain
by Amazon